# Workl

Jim Kwik's

# Limitless

### Upgrade Your Brain, Learn Anything Faster, and Unlock Your Exceptional Life

Intensive Life Publishing

# Summary & Analysis

## By

## **Freeda Tao**

# Table of Contents

# Note to Readers

This is an unofficial workbook for Jim Kwik's *Limitless: Upgrade Your Brain, Learn Anything Faster, and Unlock Your Exceptional Life* designed to enrich your reading experience. Buy the original book by visiting the link or by scanning the QR code below.

https://link.intensivelife.com/Limitless

As a way of saying **THANK YOU**,

we are offering a **FREE** copy of *Summary of Untamed*.

You will also be part of our **Readers Circle**!

Just visit the link or scan the QR code below:

https://link.intensivelife.com/free

# How to Use This Workbook

This workbook serves as a companion to the source material and provides you with helpful insight and additional information that is professionally crafted to help you better understand the content of the original work. This workbook also includes a series of reflective questions that would help you assess and evaluate your current situation as well as reflect on what you have absorbed while reading the book.

When reading this workbook, you will encounter background information about the author and his writing. We have also crafted a summary overview of the book that highlights some key ideas without revealing specific details.

We have also added analysis sections for each chapter and some original samples that will give you a further insight concerning your reading. At the end of each chapter, you will encounter takeaways that will provide you with further knowledge, reflective questions that will help you remember what you have learned, and tips that will aid you in planning your next steps. Finally, action steps are also included to remind you of the important things you need to do to make the most out of the original text.

This workbook is not created as a substitute for the original work. Instead, this will serve as a companion to it to help readers maximize the data gathered, and upgrade their knowledge and understanding to an even higher level.

# *Limitless* Workbook Overview

Jim had an accident at a very young age and suffered brain damage, affecting his learning ability. In an amazing turn of events, he became a brain expert and has recently written a uniquely and intelligently crafted book. Jim Kwik's *Limitless: Upgrade Your Brain, Learn Anything Faster, And Unlock Your Exceptional Life* shows readers how powerful the human brain is. It puts forth the idea that everyone can optimize their brain and awaken the true genius within.

The book received generous feedback from personalities like Will Smith, Tom Bilyeu, Jack Canfield, and Quincy Jones. 17-time Grand Slam winner tennis star, Novak Djokovic, even described Jim's work as "empowering, *Limitless* will take you to places you never expected."

In the book, Jim describes humans as superheroes of their own story, and just like superheroes, there is no limit to our capacity since we all have the resources we need. If we know how to tap it and bring out that genius within us, we are limitless. The only limit we have is our imagination. Why should we let small obstacles in our lives stop us from achieving unimaginable feats? In this book, Kwik shares the user manual of the greatest, most complex technology ever created—our brain. We can learn and realize how we should use our brains more efficiently and effectively. This book also underlines the methods we can use to remember everything we read, from articles to books. Kwik helps people in realizing the wrong dogmas of our society, which affects not only the young generation but also the general working of it all. He shows readers that people are making the same mistakes again and again, leading them to be less productive.

The foreword, written by Dr. Mark Hyman—an American physician and a 13-time New York Times bestselling author—elevates this book even more. Mark Hyman has been known for being passionate about wellness and functional medicine, transforming the food system, and encouraging policy change for the sake of better Public health. Hyman outlines the four main villains of our society that have been fed by too much reliance on technology:

1.  Digital Deluge
2.  Digital Distraction
3.  Digital Dementia
4.  Digital Deduction

The combined effect of these villains robs us of our power to achieve anything great, and more importantly, robs us of our ability to clearly and truly think. Kwik highlights the importance of the health and fitness of our brain through this book. The mind needs exercise as much as the body, and Jim is the living example of someone who has changed the way he uses his brain entirely.

The book is divided into four parts. In the first part of the book, Jim gives us a baseline of the wonderful possibilities of becoming limitless. He provides great insights from his research and personal experiences that motivated him to shift his mindset. First, readers have to start asking the right questions and free themselves of labels placed on them by other people.

**Chapter 1. Becoming Limitless.** Jim walks us through his life and how it changed after an accident impacted his brain development. In this chapter, Jim gives readers an endearing image of him growing up. He speaks about being imprisoned by other people's perceptions of him as a "boy with a broken brain." Growing up, Jim was good at being invisible. He was limited from doing anything because he was trapped in careless statements made by others. Jim points out the power of words and how external words can become internalized by children and rob them of the experience of unraveling their full potential. Jim was trapped for several years until he finally felt that these limitations had to stop. He thought there has to be a better way to learn. He realized that becoming limitless was not just about accelerated learning and having an incredible memory; it's all about stepping beyond what the programming world tells you. In taking the first step to becoming limitless, Jim also expresses the importance of having a *Limitless Model*, one that will serve as a guide to ensure you don't get sidetracked and controlled by false perceptions.

**Chapter 2. Why This Matters Now.** Kwik says that every human being has his own superpower, and just like in every film or series, there is always a villain. In his book, he identified the four villains to every superhero. He also pointed out that just like every antagonist we see in movies, they all started as good people before they become the bad guys. Something happened along the way that changed them. He shared how these villains have contributed to the advancement of our technology at the present times. However, though they are helpful to us, they also tend to amplify distraction and sleeplessness. He named the four villains as digital deluge, digital distraction, digital dementia, and digital deduction.

**Chapter 3. Your Limitless Brain.** Jim argues that a human brain is much better than any other device and unfathomably valuable if we only know how to maximize its full potential. Did you know that our brains could generate 70,000 thoughts per day? Unsurprisingly, unless we choose our thoughts carefully, it can be quite stressful. Our brain is what makes us different from animals. We cannot breathe in water or even fly based on our nature, but we can create something that will help us breathe in water and fly. There is no age limit to enhancing your brain's capacity; you always have the power to tap your inner genius. Our brain works like a muscle: the more you use it, the more it improves your brainpower. In the book, Jim links our gut with our brain, presenting it as our second brain. You usually feel this when you experience butterflies in your stomach. Each and every one of us has experienced some sort of a gut feeling, and it sometimes saves us from danger. To explain how our brain and gut (located in the stomach) are interrelated, Jim explains that both use the same nerves to communicate with each other. This is the key to tapping the superpower in our heads. At this point, all you need is to decide to use it to achieve your goals.

**Chapter 4. How to Read and Remember This (and Any) Book.** In this chapter, Jim explains that humans tend to forget almost half of what they learn in just an hour. On average, 70% of people forget what they have learned within 24 hours, something psychologists refer to as the *Forgetting Curve*. This is where Jim's expertise comes in, providing readers with strategies that they can apply to whatever activities they do. In this chapter, he introduces the *Pomodoro Technique*. He explains the nature of the human attention span and why Pomodoro is effective in learning. If you are someone who tends to procrastinate before a test, then you better change your habits and your strategies, as cramming will not get you the grades, and your brain will not be able to retain information. When you use the Pomodoro Technique, taking breaks is actually important because you will be able to retain far more of what you have studied than when you cram. Additionally, the act of reading a book can actually help accelerate your learning ability. You just need to commit to learning FASTER and ask the right questions as you go.

The second part takes us to the "Limitless Mindset." Here, Jim discusses how our mindset is influenced by the people around us and the kind of environment we have been accustomed to. Studies show that environmental factors play an important role in a child's development. Basically, a child develops his or her own set of beliefs based on the kind of relationships he or she has or the kind of culture he or she is exposed to. These *Belief Systems* that we have developed over the years have become our program, and it seems difficult to break from them. Jim gives us insight into how to break away from the old patterns that have imprisoned us and tap our highest potential. Thus, in this part of the book, get ready to unlearn the learned helplessness, and start understanding how to be limitless.

**Chapter 5. The Spell of Belief Systems.** This chapter provides readers with insights into why superheroes do not give in to limiting beliefs. Superman, Iron Man, and Captain Marvel are superheroes with superpowers that make them fearless in going about their role of saving the universe. Captain Marvel was never troubled with the idea of roaming in space alone because there are no restrictions when you have superpowers. Jim always points out that we are superheroes with superpowers, and you need to only realize your own power to start creating a superhero mindset. So, how do you overpower limiting beliefs? It pays to recognize when we are falling for the trap of false beliefs. Be aware of your thoughts and your beliefs as they will deprive you of the amazing possibilities. According to Jim, one solution that could help in overpowering your limiting beliefs is self-talking and motivation. When a thought tries to occupy your mind, talk it out and try to signal your brain that beliefs are of no use and need to be filtered out. The brain will do its job. There is power in positivity. Jim shared a study where it was proven that people who are happy generally see more possibilities present in the world. He added that positivity does not only benefit you but the people around you as well.

**Chapter 6. The 7 Lies of Learning.** Jim discusses the 7 LIEs (*Limited Ideas Entertained*) that make us helpless as we go about our life journey. Their formation started during our childhood. The child got it from his or her environment, parents, or some other daily factors during childhood. These are sets of programs that seemed to be the norm for our society. The full details of these sets of LIEs will be discussed in the analysis portion of this summary.

- LIE: Intelligence is fixed

- LIE: We only use 10% of our brain

- LIE: Mistakes are failures

- LIE: Knowledge is power

- LIE: Learning new things is difficult

- LIE: The criticism of other people matters

- LIE: Genius is born

These lies have limited us from seeing more Einsteins every single day. Jim has provided useful tips on putting a stop to these LIEs and taking back control.

The third part of the book is all about "Limitless Motivation." This portion dives deeper into the WHY. Jim explains what makes a person do unwanted things. Tom Bilyeu, one of Jim's friends, doesn't like working out, yet he does it anyway, all because he has a deeper why. He is compelled to keep going because the effects of working out are valuable. Jim explains that motivation is not something that we have; it is something that we do. It is a process that we have control over if we know the right recipes. Jim presents a formula that could help you obtain sustainable motivation. It is a matter of purpose, energy, and small simple steps.

**Chapter 7. Purpose.** Jim walks us back to his childhood, what drove his motivation at that time to compensate for his lacking abilities, and how hard it was to prove that despite being handicapped, he was capable. He shares that as he witnessed himself advance his level of capacity, his purpose also changed. He continued to work hard and level up despite the challenges he had to go through of constantly feeling exhausted, sleep-deprived, and of course, having to defy his extreme introvert nature to spread his discoveries. His main purpose is to help others improve their learning capacity in the same way that he did without having to suffer like him. How do you know your purpose? It's all about digging deeper into your being and asking 'WHY?' It's when you know your purpose that you truly know who you are. When you know yourself, everything else will follow.

**Chapter 8. Energy.** Jim discusses how having clarity of purpose should be accompanied with limitless brain energy. Jim wrote this book to maximize our full potential without us having to suffer in the same way that he did. In this chapter, Jim outlines ten tips in generating our limitless energy, and two of the ten recommendations he mentions include sleep and brain food. He shares that lack of sleep can trigger a lot of illnesses. Jim shares that people who don't have enough sleep suffer through depression, fatigue, and exhaustion. Meditation can be your friend to improve your sleep. Meditation has been used by different sectors of our society. Some use it for weight loss, some for healing, and some for spiritual purposes. Regardless of the intention, meditation has been proven to have a great positive effect on the individual when correctly utilized. Jim points out that fueling your brain is important to becoming limitless. With simple steps, it can bring huge change.

**Chapter 9. Small Simple Steps.** In this chapter, it's all about moving forward regardless of how little your steps are. It is a common fact that humans tend to procrastinate when we are set to do something big. It appears that individuals get overwhelmed with the number of things to be done.

When this happens, Jim reminds us to be kind to ourselves, never give ourselves a hard time, and rather, give ourselves a tap on the back, reminding ourselves that it's okay to start with simple little steps. Establishing a habit starts in baby steps, perhaps you wanted to finish reading this book because you wanted to finish reading five books in a month. But as mentioned, reading the book in one sitting might get you overwhelmed and even lead you to forget what you have read. So simple steps could get you further along and establish a habit of reading. When you keep on repeating a simple step, you suddenly go on autopilot, and you actually gain a habit.

**Chapter 10. Flow.** Being in the flow state seems to boost one's productivity. To be in that state means to have an intense focus on something and not getting distracted by the world around. It's like being shielded from the noise and other interrupting factors and not noticing any interruptions at all. However, not everyone gets into that state successfully. In the book, Jim provides us tips on how to find our flow when we really need it. In the book, Jim presents five ways of finding flow.

**Eliminate Distractions** - In the real world, you can expect distractions from other people: from the sound of the gadgets around you and sometimes even from your own thoughts. According to Jim, once you get distracted from the flow, it can take 20 minutes to get back to that state again. So, start by eliminating distractions before you even begin.

**Give yourself enough time** - Never pressure yourself to get into the flow, because it will just overwhelm you and get you frustrated. It cannot be forced, but it can be channeled. Give yourself two hours to be in that state of flow if you must. Do not rush.

21

**Do something you love** - When you are doing something you love, it's easy to get in the flow because nothing is forced, and you are doing something that matters to you.

**Have clear goals** – Clarity is important in any situation. It is important that you are clear about what you want to achieve at a given time.

**Challenge yourself... a little** – Do something you love but take on the challenges that accompany it. You won't get frustrated easily because what you are doing is something valuable to you.

We have reached the fourth part of the book, "Limitless Method." Now that we know the whys and we understood the nature of our purpose, it's time for the HOW. Jim puts emphasis on how methods play an essential role in paving the way to being limitless. In the context of this book, the method is the process of learning how to learn. Jim shares the science of accelerated areas: focus, study, increasing your memory, speed-reading, and thinking. When reading the next five chapters, take notice of the lead-in-questions and exercises found in the original book.

**Chapter 11. Focus.** Have you ever recalled one vivid event in your life when you were so engrossed in doing something that it felt like you were the only person in the world? Were you just amazed at how focused you were and how you got good feedback on the work? Focus is something that helps you get things done in the right way. To retain that focus, you should always consider eliminating any forms of distraction. If you're someone who easily loses focus, this chapter is valuable for you. It takes practice and dedication to concentrate. So, where do we start? Start with daily things. If you are writing, focus on that task and give all your attention to it. Directing your focus on a single activity is a good method to exercise your ability to concentrate. Remember, one of the enemies of flow is multitasking; this method is not only inefficient but could also lead you to disaster when it comes to your output. It is important to focus on one task at a time. Declutter your environment when necessary because a filthy and disorganized environment sends the signal of chaos to the brain that could affect your productivity.

**Chapter 12. Study.** We are all made to believe that we already know what it takes to learn. But Jim points out that the learning strategies we gathered as children are not as effective as the method this chapter is about to share. Most of the students default to cramming when studying. He explains that the human brain only absorbs 20% of what students learn within 24 hours. Jim illustrates the benefit of the Pomodoro Technique, a time management method that breaks down your tasks into intervals to make you more productive. Jim mentions that if you can increase your competence level, then you can cultivate that power of learning how to absorb a subject in one sitting using the different tools Jim has presented. In this particular chapter, you will learn about the four levels of competence backed by psychology. The goal is to reach the level of unconscious competence where a certain skill is already in your nature; it's like you are on autopilot. Jim feels that another level of competence should be added, a level of being limitless that he terms as 'True Mastery.' To be on that level, according to Jim, one needs to study like a superhero.

**Chapter 13. Memory.** Jim says that memory is one of our greatest assets. It supports us in every aspect of our lives. You can't do anything without it. And it works like a muscle; the more you use it, the stronger it gets. He says that there is no such thing as a bad memory or a good memory; there is only a trained and an untrained brain. Memory can be increased and decreased by how much you practice it. Memory retention is essential, and that is why Jim presents four methods that can help memory retention.

**Visualization** – whether you just want to increase memory retention or manifest something, this method makes a certain matter easier to remember.

**Association** – according to Jim, this is the key to remembering. Whenever you look at something, you remember any association you have of it.

**Emotion** – according to Jim, whenever there's emotion involved in a memory, it gets more deeply embedded.

And finally, **location** – We don't need to remember numbers and words if there are locations present.

**Chapter 14. Speed Reading.** Since the early chapters of this book, Jim has been consistent with sharing the importance of reading. Jim explains that reading improves our focus, our memory, our vocabulary, slows the aging process, and, more importantly, reduces Alzheimer's by 60%. Further, reading also improves imagination. There are many things that prevent speed reading such as regression or mind wandering—when you're reading a line but you have to read it again and again because your mind keeps wandering somewhere else. The second thing is outdated skills. Jim says that we haven't been taught how to read since the 4<sup>th</sup> or 5<sup>th</sup> grades. Third, we speak every word as we read. He emphasizes that repeating every word in your brain slows the speed-reading process immensely. These are the primary obstacles in our speed reading. Jim provides us with solutions on how we could enhance our speed-reading ability. For regression, he shares that we should read the book with our fingers on the line we're reading. It keeps our minds from wandering. For outdated skills, Jim encourages us to continuously practice and increase our reading speed by setting a timer for two minutes and then analyzing how many words we have read by using a detailed formula he mentions in the book. And for obstacles, we should read with images and visualization. Jim encourages us to keep these solutions in mind and apply them to our daily reading.

**Chapter 15. Thinking.** You have heard the adage "think outside the box." But Jim contradicts this line and says that we should think in another box altogether as this improves efficiency. How does it work? He quotes Albert Einstein's philosophy: *"We can't solve problems by using the same kind of thinking we used when we created them."* Jim finds this posit to be sensible. He mentions that perspectives should be challenged from time to time in order to confirm if they are still viable or not. It is important to note that challenges are often the consequences of a particular way of thinking; presenting a new perspective or a fresh approach to the table can be the only practical way to solve the problem. Kwik also presents us with *mental models*. He says that mental models are the shortcut to decoding the world around us and making sense of everything. Mental models train your mind to think.

# Chapter by Chapter Analysis

In the succeeding pages of this book summary, some key ideas from Jim Kwik's *Limitless* are combined with relevant research and analysis.

# Part 1: Free Your Mind

## Chapter 1: Becoming Limitless

**The Limitless Model.** In this chapter, Jim presents the Limitless Model that will serve as the framework of his book. Through this model, readers will learn how to have a Limitless Mindset, Limitless Motivation, and Limitless Method.

In the book, Jim shares his difficulty when it came to learning. He became the weird kid in school and an outcast and was bullied. Jim even recalls an instance when a teacher was so frustrated about Jim not able to comprehend the lesson that she blurted out *"This is the boy with a broken brain,"* a statement that he then internalized. That statement imprisoned him into thinking he was defective. He found comfort in reading Marvel comics. It was the only thing that helped him learn to read. He was fascinated with the idea of superheroes, considering himself invisible. It was his superpower. This personal story reminds us to be mindful of the words we tell children, making sure that what we tell them does not become a long-lasting limiting belief.

Stan Lee's X-Men superheroes and Albert Einstein were misunderstood and not able to fit in, something Jim could relate to. Before the X-Men became superheroes, they were outcasts and were not accepted by society. The famous Albert Einstein was referred to as someone who had a problem speaking; it was said that he had the habit of repeating words to himself. Thus, he was perceived as someone with a speech problem, autism, dyslexia, and schizophrenia. Yet, he turned out to be a genius. Reading these comics and reading about Albert Einstein's biography gave Jim hope that someday he could overcome his challenges.

Jim managed to get into college, but his journey was never easy. He planned to drop out, but a friend talked him out of it and invited Jim to spend time with his family. This was the beginning of the tipping point for him. The friend's father gave him three books to read. Reading was such a challenge for Jim that he found it difficult to juggle his school activities and keeping his promise to read the books. This ended Jim in the hospital.

At this point, Jim finally started to ask the right questions and came to the realization that he needed to learn how to learn.

Jim studied his condition to understand how his brain worked. He soon observed some changes in his brain while he was learning new concepts. He had a stronger ability to focus than before. He was able to break free from the limiting belief that used to imprison him, and it was replaced by a more positive outlook. He started to believe that anything was possible. Over time, Jim felt the need to share his discoveries with others and help people unlock their own exceptional life, especially those children who have learning disabilities and those older individuals who have an aging brain. In the span of 20 years, Jim Kwik has made it his mission to *"build better, brighter brains."* Indeed, it was a remarkable journey for Jim. He later learned that becoming limitless is not just about accelerated learning and having an incredible memory; it's all about stepping beyond what the world tells you. In taking the first step to becoming limitless, Jim also expressed the importance of having a model that would serve as one's guide to ensure they didn't get sidetracked and controlled by perceived limitations.

## The Takeaway

What keeps us from reaching our highest potential are the limiting beliefs we have imprisoned ourselves within. Evaluating where you are at this moment in your life and acknowledging your weakness is a good start. Visualizing what you want to achieve is a perfect start to becoming limitless. There is some sort of truth in this line from William Hutchison Murray: *"...the moment you commit yourself into something, providence moves too."* Jim is the living example that anything is possible.

## Points for Reflection

What is it about Jim's story that you feel you can relate to?

_Challenges in focus_

_Overcoming individual's words_

Why is it important to be mindful of what we say to children?

_Your words can create limiting_

_beliefs_

What are your limiting beliefs?

_I ride horses only at a certain level_

_My writing is wordy/slow_

_I don't have value to earn 6 figures_

_Unfocussed Reader_

_I'll never achieve my goal weight_

_/fitness goals are plateaued._

_Boundary level/hd design options are_

_not available._

## *Goals*

Being aware of what keeps you from becoming limitless, what do you think you would do to break that perceived limitations that have shaped your journey?

- Sports Psychology
- Recruitment Agencies, Pursuing New Career Paths
- Cont'd writing for CCE and/or Reports

Where do you think you should start your journey to becoming limitless?

- Reading → Making time for focus
- Researching career options
- Signing up w/ Recruitment Agency
- Banking & form d... ...
- Stretching daily → mind & body

1. **VISUALIZATION**. Take time to visualize your dream and the things you want to achieve. Create a vision board, if necessary, to remind you of your goals.

# Chapter 2: Why This Matters Now

Jim believes that we are all superheroes with superpowers. We may not have the same superpowers as those famous superheroes, but in the real world, we can make things possible by accelerating our brainpower. However, just like superheroes, we also have our enemies. Jim refers to these as **Digital Deluge**, **Digital Distraction**, **Digital Dementia**, and **Digital Deduction**.

**Digital Deluge.** Today, it is easy to gather information, and there is so much to process. According to research, *"an average person consumes three times as much information as one did in the 1960s."* The effect of digital deluge on our minds is causing us to be unproductive and limited when it comes to absorbing new information. This is how the deluge of data is affecting us. Thus, it is important to note that downtime is necessary to refresh our thoughts and encourage creativity. Give yourself 30 minutes a day to not think of anything and to keep away from using technology. Perhaps having a 30-minute meditation would be a good start since meditation has been proven to help relax our minds.

**Digital Distraction.** We are consumed by our phones. We are engrossed in checking our social media. People are developing social media addictions. As Jim points, we love the idea of always staying connected because we feel secure; however, it does not make us happier. It is said that an excessive amount of dopamine can lead to hallucinations and schizophrenia. That is why multitasking is not effective when we want to maximize our brain. Taking a break from our phone on a daily basis is a good way of not being sidetracked. Perhaps it's time to gain a sense of discipline.

**Digital Dementia.** Digital dementia happens when we overuse technology and decrement our cognitive ability. We learn the most when we participate in the process of learning. According to research, the more you use your brain, the stronger it gets and can absorb and store information better. So, it is important to do not waste your brain's storage and store only what matters. According to Jim, either you use it or lose it. You choose.

**Digital Deduction.** The fourth horseman is robbing us of our liberty to formulate thoughts, opinions, and make decisions; yet we're not even aware of it. We are relying on the internet for almost everything, and we lose the opportunity to reflect and draw conclusions of our own experience or knowledge. Simply put, we let the internet decide it for us.

How do we fight against these? Be mindful of your learning process. Jim says that he loves to use social media, likes to connect with people, empower them. But fire can either cook for you or burn your house; it depends on how you use it. Technology is similar to that. It is a good servant; however, it can be a terrible one.

## The Takeaway

When you decide to become limitless, opportunities to level up your consciousness follow. This is one important tool you will probably use as you live a limitless life. When you are conscious of your actions and situations, it will be easy to recognize the supervillains. It is important to note that technology is good when used in the right away. Anything in excess is considered bad for one's mental health.

## *Points for Reflection*

What have you understood about these digital villains?

_____

_____

_____

_____

_____

Can you recall a point in your life when you have encountered any of these digital villains? How did they affect you?

_____

_____

_____

_____

_____

Why do you think consciousness is important in becoming limitless?

_____

_____

_____

_____

_____

*Goals*

How would you make use of technology without risking your mental health?

_____

_____

_____

_____

_____

What are the necessary adjustments that you should make given the effect of the four horsemen on your mental health? How would you keep things balanced?

_____

_____

_____

_____

_____

1. **CREATING A HABIT**. Start a habit of taking time away from technology for at least 30 minutes every week. Allot this time to doing something creative or simple. Do something that would help you relax. Turn off your phone when you need to. Relax and be creative.

# Chapter 3: Your Limitless Brain

Jim points out that we have an important asset that could create wonders—our brains. The human brain is different from that of animals. Humans can't breathe in water or fly on their own, but we can use our brains to create tools or ways to make breathing in water or flying possible. Did you know that there is no age limit for brain development? Our brains have neuroplasticity, and that may simply be the reason why Jim was able to turn his life around and become a brain expert. Jim's recovery may be perceived as a miracle, but in truth, cases like Jim's have proven that we have the ability to heal through neuroplasticity. Neuroplasticity also plays an essential role in our ability to learn.

The principle is that our experiences shape our brains. That is why Jim puts emphasis on asking the right questions and using our brains to our advantage. Let's take programming as an example. You don't know how to code or use a programming language, so you decide to learn object-oriented programming. What do you do? You start with learning the concept of programming, you do your research and learn what you feel you need to. But in order to learn, you also need to apply and do coding along the way until you master the concept and you can create your own application out of the basic principles. Over time, you start being on autopilot when it comes to coding because you have mastered it and practiced it on a regular basis. You increase your brainpower. We become what we think and do.

By now, it is already clear that we have the power to turn things around. And if the constant dilemma is forgetfulness, distraction, and the feeling of inadequacy, it's about time to change your mindset by thinking the right thoughts. Negative pep talk about yourself can create limiting beliefs that affect your attitude towards any situation. So, choose your thoughts carefully.

*The Takeaway*

If those who went through major brain injuries were able to turn their lives around and use their weakness to reset, then so can anyone. We also have the power to become limitless. Being limitless is a choice: Will you take a step outside your comfort zone and discover how to unravel your own power? Or will you stay where you are, trapped and shackled by the limiting beliefs that others projected on you? You choose.

Can you recall a time when you believed other people's perceived notions about you? How did it make you feel?

_____

_____

_____

_____

_____

If you had to choose between the red pill and the blue pill in the Matrix, which one would you choose? Why?

_____

_____

_____

_____

_____

*Goals*

Why do you think it's important to be mindful of your thoughts?

_____

_____

_____

_____

_____

Choosing your thoughts impacts your brain. Given that whatever you think could make or break you, how can you train yourself to choose the right thoughts?

_____

_____

_____

_____

_____

Now that you know that you have the power to live an exceptional life by having a limitless brain, what will be your next step?

_____

_____

_____

_____

_____

1. **DECIDE**. In order to become limitless, you must first decide to accept the challenge of conquering your limiting beliefs.

2. **CHOOSE YOUR THOUGHTS**. Remember, "As a man thinketh, so is he."

3. **TRUST YOUR GUT FEEL**.

# Chapter 4: How to Read and Remember This (and Any) Book

The previous three chapters condition our mind to be open to possibilities based on the data backed by scientific discoveries. In the succeeding chapters, Jim provides tools that we could apply as we go about improving our memory.

Let's meet Tina and Miah. They go to the same class every day and get the same information. However, since they are both unique individuals with unique neurons, they absorb information differently. On a regular basis, Tina is consistent when it comes to learning; she makes it a point to always read and write down her thoughts after she learns something. Tina follows the Pomodoro Technique, a mechanism developed for productivity. Tina spends 25 minutes on reading and learning then takes a 5-minute break after every 25 minutes of studying. She is able to develop this habit, and it works well for her. On the day of the exam, she doesn't need to cram; in fact, she just reviews and follows the Pomodoro Technique. Miah, on the other hand, is also very diligent. However, she tends to study for a longer length of time without breaks, which leads to exhaustion.

What are the differences? Although both were studious and diligent, Tina still scores higher in the exam. Why? Tina has made use of the Pomodoro Technique, which helps her to better absorb the things she needs to learn. She absorbs information better than Miah because Tina was able to take advantage of both primacy and recency. Jim explains that the effect of primacy is that one is likely to learn at the beginning of a lesson, while recency's effect is that one is likely to remember the last part of the lesson. Tina is able to maximize her learning because she gets to take advantage of the effects of recency and primacy by using the Pomodoro method in learning.

Kwik presents us with a terminology called FASTER:

- **F is for Forget.** Forget every unnecessary item and limitations that define you. Think of yourself as limitless. You can do everything. It helps to talk to yourself positively and be receptive to new learning.
- **A is for Act.** What promotes learning is taking notes, highlight every idea that you come across. Exercise before the class begins. These are the little ways that help promote productivity and boost memory and cognitive skills.
- **S is for State.** Studies prove that if a person is depressed, they are less likely to remember anything, whereas if the person is excited or joyful, they remember many details about a specific event. Jim says that we should change the depth of our breathing or change our posture because all the learning we do is state-dependent.
- **T is for Teach.** When you teach something, you learn it twice: once with yourself, and then again when you are teaching another person.

- **E is for Enter.** Make use of your calendar and jot down important things in your schedule. Include your personal growth and development. Remember that if it's not in the calendar, it's not getting done.
- **R is for Review.** Actively recall what you have learned with spaced intervals.

By adhering to these principles, you are taking a big step towards accelerating your brain's capacity. Commitment is important if you want to see a remarkable improvement.

## The Takeaway

It always boils down to choosing to commit to becoming limitless. This chapter has provided you with an effective method to accelerate your brain's learning power. It's up to you to take advantage of it. Ask the right questions every time you encounter something new: *How can I use this? Why must I use this? When will I use this?*

*Points for Reflection*

Do you believe that you can improve your brain's learning power? Why?

_____

_____

_____

_____

_____

Where are you at this point in your journey to accelerating your brain-power?

_____

_____

_____

_____

_____

Could Jim's 'FASTER' principles in learning be beneficial in your journey towards becoming limitless? Why?

_____

_____

_____

_____

_____

*Goals*

How can you make use of the primacy and recency of learning?

_____

_____

_____

_____

_____

Do you think taking notes is an important tool that you can apply to your daily learning activities? Why or why not?

_____

_____

_____

_____

_____

How would you apply the Pomodoro Technique and note-taking to your learning process?

_____

_____

_____

_____

_____

1. Apply the '**FASTER**' principle in learning. Observe any signs of improvement.

2. The **POMODORO TECHNIQUE**. Integrate this mechanism when learning new things.

# Part 2: Limitless Mindset: The What

## Chapter 5: The Spell of Belief Systems

What keeps us from becoming our own superhero is our belief system that has been controlling us since we were kids. These limiting beliefs were developed through the people around us, the kind of environment that we grew up in, and the set of values instilled by our parents. In this chapter, Jim presents reflective questions:

**Why do our beliefs have such an effect on our lives?**

These limiting beliefs and self-consciousness are revealed when you talk to yourself. You want to become that great person you dreamt about since forever, but there is a voice telling you that you cannot do it, and you do not have the skills or qualifications. We listen to these false beliefs and are unable to achieve greatness in our lives. This is what false beliefs do to us.

When we first arrive in this world, we are unaware of anything. Our parents are the ones who are our first mentors, guides, and teachers. They mean no harm to us, but sometimes we are limited by the wrong belief systems that they have inscribed upon us.

Jim shares the story of a lady who moved to a new country, but she wasn't prepared to experience its culture. She struggled for ten years just to be part of the society. Throughout her journey, she was mocked and was made fun of, all because she couldn't speak the language. This mockery and ridicule became her perceived limitation, and she couldn't aspire for anything greater. One day, she decided to face the battle. And just like that, she is now known as the co-founder of a very large institute which has served big companies like Nike and SpaceX, among others. She basically shifted from someone with a limited mindset to someone who believes that she can change and shape her mind to achieve her goals.

**Why do limiting beliefs keep you from your goals?**

We tend to see limiting beliefs as our reality. We have lived with them for a long period of time, and reshaping our mindset doesn't just happen overnight. We are controlled by the thoughts that are causing us to doubt our capacity. Limiting beliefs are already instilled in our minds, convincing us that we don't deserve something remarkable and good. We cannot perceive ourselves as geniuses because we feel we are not capable. These beliefs become voices in our heads, telling us that we are no good and that we will never succeed. The truth is, we are all geniuses. Being a genius is not limited to having a high IQ. Jim shares that being a genius comes in different forms:

- **Dynamo geniuses** are those who have the ability to express themselves through creativity and ideas, such as Shakespeare.
- **Blaze geniuses** are those who know how to convey their story and connect with people and their hearts, such as Oprah.
- **Tempo geniuses** are those who know how to see the light at the end of the tunnel and see the wisdom, such as Nelson Mandela.
- **Steel geniuses** are those who process information in bulk, see small things that other people didn't notice, and use the data to create something great, much like how Sergey Brin co-founded Google.

Your genius could be a combination of these geniuses. You could have the dynamo like Shakespeare while you also possess the Blaze just like Oprah. Jim points out that there is some combination of genius inside all of us. We just have to allow it to express itself.

### How do you reject limiting beliefs?

In order to reject limiting beliefs and develop a superhero mindset, Jim gives readers three keys: (a) name your limiting beliefs, (b) get to the facts, and (c) create a new belief.

**Key 1: Name your Limiting Beliefs.** Pay attention to the inner voices. It has been part of your programming to bully yourself by believing how incapable you are. If you are aware of the limiting phrases you tell yourself, then you can get rid of them easier.

**Key 2: Get to the Facts.** Recall an event when you had to do something but were triggered by your limiting belief. Instead of focusing on the emotion, try to recall the experience and how the event went. This allows you to evaluate your life experiences.

**Key 3: Create a new Belief.** When you have already identified your limiting beliefs and assessed the events that took place due to those beliefs, you need to send a signal to your brain that these kinds of thoughts hinder you and should be filtered out.

One can only discover one's greatest potential if one truly commits to fight against limiting beliefs. It pays to be mindful of different events taking place that trigger limiting beliefs echoing in your head. You are larger than these. Don't let them imprison you from doing something that could reveal your exceptional life.

*Points for Reflection*

What are the limiting beliefs that have impacted you?

_____

_____

_____

_____

_____

What are the instances or situations in your life that trigger these limiting beliefs?

_____

_____

_____

_____

_____

Do you intend to fight your limiting beliefs?

_____

_____

_____

_____

_____

What does it take to have a superhero mindset?

_____

_____

_____

_____

_____

What form or combination of geniuses are you?

_____

_____

_____

_____

_____

1. **POSITIVE MINDSET**. Start a habit of having a positive mindset. It will not only help you manage stress and keep you from possible health risks, but it will also open up new possibilities.

# Chapter 6: The 7 Lies of Learning

**Lie #1: Intelligence is fixed.** Since childhood, we are programmed to believe that intelligence is fixed and cannot be developed over time. According to Jim, intelligence is the combination of attitudes and actions. Thus, intelligence is fluid.

**Lie #2: We only use 10% of our brains.** This myth is false. We have been made to believe for a long time that we only use a small portion of our brain. The fact is, we use 100% of our brains. Some just use their brain better than others. It is important to learn how to use your brain as efficiently and effectively as possible.

**Lie #3: Mistakes are failures.** In school, we are expected to be competitive and to ace tests. We have been conditioned to believe that mistakes mean failures. Einstein himself made hundreds of basic mistakes in his calculations. Yet, was he remembered for his mistakes or the advancements he made in physics? *"There is no such thing as failure, only failure to learn."*

**Lie #4: Knowledge is power.** It is only when knowledge is accompanied by an act that it can be considered as power. Knowledge x Action = POWER.

**Lie #5: Learning new things is difficult.** Learning is often associated with school. We remember all the difficulties, the rejection, and the emotional struggle we experienced while in school. However, as adults, if we take it one step at a time, we can become comfortable with the process of learning.

**Lie #6: The criticism of other people matters.** Wanting to please others is part of the culture. We have been consumed with the notion that what other people say defines us. If you want to be limitless, it's time to focus on the things you love to do. Do not be afraid of people's criticism.

**Lie #7: Genius is born.** We have to nurture and let the genius in all of us grow. And this happens when we commit to learn.

*The Takeaway*

Jim learned continuously with constant practice and commitment and a goal to be his own superhero. Learning is only difficult in the beginning. Your world can only change if you start letting go of the beliefs that have imprisoned you. Start letting go of these LIEs and start believing more in what you can do. Anything is possible.

*Points for Reflection*

Which of the seven LIEs seem to have really affected your life as you were growing up? Why?

_____

_____

_____

_____

_____

Do you still believe these specific LIEs?

_____

_____

_____

_____

_____

Do you believe that you are a superhero with a superpower inside you?

_____

_____

_____

_____

_____

*Goals*

After reading this chapter, how will you address criticism?

_____

_____

_____

_____

_____

If you did not worry about people's opinions and who you are was the only thing that mattered, what would your life be like?

_____

_____

_____

_____

_____

1. **Knowledge x Action = Power**. Anything that you have learned today, put it into action and see how you are able to turn that knowledge into power.

# Part 3: Limitless Motivation: The Why

## Chapter 7: Purpose

What drives motivation is having a clear sense of purpose. If you don't have a clear vision or purpose of why you are doing something you are doing, it will be difficult to tap into motivation. Jim points out that motivation is not about doing something you enjoy but about doing that particular thing because it brings you closer to your goals.

In this chapter, Jim outlines what you need in order to get motivated. It's not every day that we feel motivated to do something, yet what makes motivation work is that inner knowing that you are basically working on something that you love.

Kwik says that hidden behind every challenge is a gift. That gift provides you with what you need to move forward. You should become very clear about your purpose, your identity, your values, and your reasons. When you have this figured out, motivation comes to you automatically.

In order to achieve goals, one needs to be smart about them. You need to be specific, the goal itself should be realistic, actionable, measurable, and it should be time-based. You should give yourself a deadline on when you are going to finish it. Moreover, these goals should not affect your health. If they're making you unhealthy and are taking your will power away from you, then you should take smaller steps.

**What is your Purpose?** Purpose is how you use your passion to help others. For example, your passion could be playing the piano, but your purpose is to make other people hear it. Whenever you wake up, you'll be ready and excited to share your piano skills with other people.

Regardless of anything, discerning your purpose starts with your *WHY*. If you ever have to do something, ask yourself, why are you doing this? If you have a deeper foundation of why you are doing what you are doing, then discerning your purpose becomes easy.

*Points for Reflection*

Evaluate the situation you are in right now. Why are you doing what you are doing?

_____

_____

_____

_____

_____

What is the difference between passion and purpose? How are they inter-related?

_____

_____

_____

_____

_____

Why do you think having a clear purpose is important to your journey to becoming limitless?

_____

_____

_____

_____

_____

## *Goals*

What are you passionate about?

_____

_____

_____

_____

_____

What is your purpose?

_____

_____

_____

_____

_____

1. **WHO ARE YOU?** The goal is to be conscious of who you really are. Identify your traits and qualities, even the things you want to create or establish. Start with I AM _____.

2. **ASK WHY.** Get into the habit of asking the deeper why. Why are you doing what you are doing?

# Chapter 8: Energy

Having clarity of purpose is not enough. In order to make things work, you also have to fuel your energy to maximize your brain's potential. Jim discusses that having clarity of purpose should be accompanied with limitless brain energy. He presents ten essential steps on how to fuel your energy, and three of them are sleep, brain food, and exercise.

Jim puts emphasis on the importance of having regular sleeping hours to accelerate brain capacity. We have heard and read about the importance of having enough sleep, but in this book, sleep is crucial for focus and better memory. Recent findings of having quality sleep suggest that sleeping helps cleanse toxins in your brain to start afresh when you wake up. If sleep does not come naturally to you, there are some proven techniques that Jim shares.

- Aerobic exercise for 16 weeks significantly increases sleep time.
- Meditation has also proven to be very successful.

Even just a 10-minute aerobic exercise can already have a great effect on your brain.

Apart from sleep and exercise, Jim also explains the value of eating brain food. Eating brain food has great effects on one's cognitive ability. Should you need some recipes to get you started, Jim shares great options in the book.

*The Takeaway*

In order to tap into our full potential, we need to fuel our energy. Just like water, sleep is crucial for mental health. Since our brain is our powerful tool for living an exceptional life, it is important to take care of it. Simple things like taking a break after a long productive day and getting enough sleep can help you reset.

*Points for Reflection*

Do you find yourself lacking sleep because you are busy? How does it affect your productivity?

_____

_____

_____

_____

_____

What exactly happens every time you don't get enough sleep?

_____

_____

_____

_____

_____

How can meditation help in your limitless journey?

_____

_____

_____

_____

_____

*Goals*

What kind of food should you include in your diet to benefit your brain health?

_____

_____

_____

_____

_____

What would be your next steps in ensuring that you are taking care of your brain health?

_____

_____

_____

_____

_____

1. **MEDITATE**. Incorporate at least a 10-15-minute daily meditation in your routine to improve your mind power.
2. **PLAN**. Establish a schedule and incorporate new activities into your calendar.
3. **SLEEP**. It is vital that you get a decent amount of sleep.
4. **DO NOT CRAM**. Practice the Pomodoro Technique instead.

# Chapter 9: Small Simple Steps

Do you encounter procrastination every once in a while, especially when you want to achieve something big? Procrastination is incorrectly linked to laziness. Procrastination is quite complex and is triggered by various factors like anxiety, mental exhaustion, ADHD, depression, or fear of failure.

Procrastination happens when we are going for something big, and we are overwhelmed with the idea that we still have so much to do. Further, it can be harmful to our health as it can have a significant effect on sleep and anxiety. Kwik says that the only thing we can do to cure this is to take small baby steps.

In order to achieve the big goal, you need to start to take small simple steps towards it. In doing so, you are reducing the amount of stress inflicted upon you. Doing one specific thing repeatedly will automatically make it your habit. Based on Jim's experience, the best way to deal with the dilemma of feeling overwhelmed with a task is to break it into mini-tasks until you finish one major task successfully.

Let's say you want to establish a minimalist lifestyle. It would be quite overwhelming to do it all at once. However, when you are really determined to transition to a minimalist lifestyle, you start gradually, perhaps by first doing your research and learning how to be a minimalist. Then, you create your own checklists based on the kind of lifestyle that you have. Let's say one of your tasks is decluttering: you should probably start with one single room, make some mini checklists of tasks to be decluttered in that specific room.

Jim also writes about the power of our DREAMS.

- **D is for Decide.** Before you go to sleep, you consciously decide that you are going to remember your dream.
- **R is for Record.** Keep a diary or a piece of paper near your bed, and whenever you wake up, write down what you remember from your dream.
- **E is for Eyes.** When remembering your dream, do not open your eyes. Opening them will lead to forgetting the dream quickly.
- **A is for Affirm.** You have to tell your brain that you need to remember your dreams when you wake up.
- **M is for Manage.** Establish good routines.
- **S stands for Share.** When you share your dreams, you can remember more of them for longer periods of time.

Jim says that if a person does these things, he can learn a lot from his dreams. Dreams are your pathways to the subconscious mind. The way you start your day defines the rest of it. Taking small steps will make your big goal easier until it no longer looks big and you have achieved it successfully.

*The Takeaway*

Taking a step towards the goal should not be hindered by moments of procrastination. When you are having trouble getting things done, remember that you can always trim it down to little pieces until you have successfully finished a daunting task.

*Points for Reflection*

How has procrastination affected your experiences?

_____

_____

_____

_____

_____

Is there something you're feeling stuck with at the moment that you want to conquer?

_____

_____

_____

_____

_____

When do you usually experience procrastination?

_____

_____

_____

_____

_____

How will you apply the simple baby steps to your dilemma?

_____

_____

_____

_____

_____

Why do you think Jim Kwik's D.R.E.A.M.S. is important for your journey to being limitless? How would you apply this to your journey?

_____

_____

_____

_____

_____

*Acton Steps*

1. In every task, always remember your deeper **WHY**.

2. Apply the **D.R.E.A.M.S.** to your journey towards being limitless and observe the difference.

# Chapter 10: Flow

Has there been a time that you were so engrossed in doing something that you forgot the world and people around you? You were so focused on a certain activity that nothing could distract or disturb you? That's called 'flow.' When you are working in the flow, your productivity increases by about five times.

Flow has eight basic characteristics: (1) absolute attention, (2) complete focus on goals, (3) the feeling that time is either speeding up or slowing down, (4) a sense of reward from that activity, (5) feeling the sense of effortlessness that as if the activity comes naturally to you, (6) the experience is not overly challenging, (7) as if your actions are on autopilot, and (8) feeling comfortable doing the task. If these eight characteristics are present when you do a specific thing, then congratulations! You have entered the state of flow.

**But how do you achieve that state of flow?**

- Eliminate distractions.
- Give yourself enough time.
- Do something you love.

- Have clear goals.

- Challenge yourself... a little.

Beware of the villains of the flow, too: stress, fear of failure, multitasking, and lack of conviction.

## The Takeaway

Being in the flow state can open possibilities, and it helps get things done faster. It is important to train yourself to achieve regular flow by trying the steps that Jim presented in the book and being aware of the enemies of flow.

*Points for Reflection*

What keeps you from achieving your flow?

_____

_____

_____

_____

_____

Can you recall a time in your life when you experienced being in the flow?
How did it go?

_____

_____

_____

_____

_____

*Goals*

What should you do to practice achieving flow?

_____

_____

_____

_____

_____

What are your ways of eliminating distractions?

_____

_____

_____

_____

_____

*Acton Steps*

1. **Create a space** where you won't get distracted; no mobile phones or anything that would keep you from achieving your flow.

# Part 4: Limitless Methods: The How

## Chapter 11: Focus

Training our brain to give all our attention to a particular activity or task is one power we can make use of to reach optimal results.

In order to train your brain to focus, we need to practice concentration. Train your brain to focus and concentrate on using the techniques shared in the book and always accompany it with eating the right food that is good for your brain and overall health. One strategy that could help is to do one task at a time. For example, when eating, concentrate on it, and do not do something else. Multitasking does not make you productive, and it will only exhaust you. So, focus on one thing at a time.

Jim shares simple necessary steps for calming our busy mind:

**Breathing.** Correct breathing is essential when it comes to our overall health. It provides mental clarity, helps in food digestion, and also improves your body's immune system.

**Eliminating the stressors.** Small simple steps are all it takes until you can do everything else with increased focus.

**Schedule time for distractions.** Jim shares that scheduling a time to deal with distractions helps in keeping your focus. One strategy is to schedule checking your phone at a specific time.

## *The Takeaway*

If you are serious about wanting to unleash your full potential, it is important to always look back to your deeper 'why' and apply the strategies that are beneficial in keeping you calm and focused. Set your schedule, divide your thoughts, and focus accordingly. Remember that it's more productive to do one thing at a time rather than multitask.

*Points for Reflection*

What keeps you distracted?

_____

_____

_____

_____

_____

Have you tried doing one task at a time? How about multitasking? Which one makes you more productive?

_____

_____

_____

_____

_____

*Goals*

Considering the insights that Jim presented in this chapter, how do you think these will benefit your daily activities?

_____

_____

_____

_____

_____

How would you apply the techniques you have learned?

_____

_____

_____

_____

_____

1. **Plan** the things you need to finish and focus on one single task at a time. Do not exercise multitasking.

# Chapter 12: Study

Jim shares that there are four levels of competence: (1) "unconscious in-competence," when you are unaware of that particular thing's existence; (2) "conscious incompetence," when you are aware that a certain thing ex-ists but have never practiced it; (3) "conscious competence," when you can perform a skill, but you can only do so when you put your mind to it; (4) and lastly, "unconscious competence," when are already on autopilot and have the ability to do a certain thing without having to fully focus. One example would be tying your shoelaces. The only way to reach the final level of com-petence is to practice that certain skill.

There are habits that we can establish in our lifelong learning:

Habit 1: Employ active recall

Habit 2: Employ spaced repetition

Habit 3: Manage the state you're in

Habit 4: Use your sense of smell

Habit 5: Music for the mind

Habit 6: Listen with your whole brain

Habit 7: Take note of taking notes

In the process of learning and ensuring you have absorbed what you have learned, it pays to apply the Pomodoro Technique while note-taking. You will be able to benefit from the primacy and recency in absorbing information. When taking notes, it is important to have a clear goal and purpose of what you want to understand. Write only the important things. This would help filter high-value information and assist you in reaching your goal.

*The Takeaway*

The whole point of wanting to maximize our brain's full potential is to be open and be able to adapt. We can maximize our learning capacity by un-learning what we used to know and adapting to the new ways and techniques of learning. Even just adapting to one habit could already make a huge difference. Do not pressure yourself; the habits presented are only tools that can help you become better in studying.

*Points for Reflection*

What are your ways of learning?

_____

_____

_____

_____

_____

Among the habits that Jim presented, which one has already been part of

your system?

_____

_____

_____

_____

_____

*Goals*

Which habit would you most likely apply in your lifelong learning? Why?

_____

_____

_____

_____

_____

If you apply any of the habits that Jim presented, how will it impact your learning process?

_____

_____

_____

_____

_____

*Acton Steps*

1. **Get into the habit** of note-taking. Write only the important things.

2. Apply the **Pomodoro Technique** when learning a new skill.

# Chapter 13: Memory

Memory is one of your greatest assets as it supports you in every aspect of your life. Memory works like a muscle; the more you use it, the stronger it gets. According to Jim, there is no such thing as good or bad memory, only a trained or an untrained brain. The thing that can help train our brain is to practice using it. He shares four methods that can contribute to increasing memory retaining time.

**Visualization.** When you want to learn something, it makes a huge difference to visualize. Learn through having a mental image of a certain thing.

**Association.** It would be good to associate something you'd like to learn with something that you already know for easier recall.

**Emotion.** It is also easier to recall information if we add an emotion to it.

**Location.** According to Jim, we are more likely to remember locations than numbers. If we learn to associate something with a place, we are more likely to remember it.

*The Takeaway*

Sometimes we need to let go and unlearn the old ways of learning and start opening our minds to new and smart ways of learning. Challenging ourselves every day when it comes to learning enhances our memory. Remember, one does not become a programmer overnight; one learns through constant practice and continuous learning.

What are the things that you need to unlearn when it comes to improving your memory?

_____

_____

_____

_____

_____

Do you always use Google when you want to learn something? Were you able to retain what you have learned from Google?

_____

_____

_____

_____

_____

## *Goals*

How do you recall a great deal of information?

_____

_____

_____

_____

_____

How can you integrate Jim's methods to improve your memory?

_____

_____

_____

_____

_____

1. **Rely on M.O.M.**, a mnemonic device that Jim created to recall memories instantly. M-for motivation, O-for observation, and M-for Methods.

# Chapter 14: Speed Reading

If you really want to tap into your exceptional life, make reading a habit. Getting into a habit of reading is an important contributing factor to becoming limitless. It does not only improve your vocabulary, but it also improves your focus, imagination, memory, and comprehension. Jim shares how we can maximize our learning process through speed reading.

**Regression** is one of the obstacles of speed reading—when one re-reads certain words with the belief that this could increase their comprehension. It disrupts the reading process and slows us down.

**Outdated skills** are another obstacle to speed reading. We also need to keep up and challenge ourselves to be able to comprehend complex materials easily.

Then there's **sub-vocalization**—when you read using your voice. Learning to read silently makes it easier for you to understand what you are reading.

For beginners, these simple steps are quite useful.

1. Read using the Pomodoro Technique.

2. Read comfortably and silently using your finger or a visual pacer.

3. When reading, integrate the methods of enhancing memory: visualization, association, emotion, and location.

4. At the end of every session, take the time to write down some notes on what you have learned.

5. Practice. There's no shortcut to becoming an expert. Practice makes you good at what you do.

*The Takeaway*

You have reached the point where you are expected to accompany your intention with actions. These are simple steps you can do as part of your daily routine. Go back to your deeper 'why' if you need to motivate yourself again. Remember the reason why you wanted to improve; remember why you want to change your life. Then go back to the exercise and do it based on what you feel you need in your life at that moment.

*Points for Reflection*

Why is reading important in accelerating our brainpower?

_____

_____

_____

_____

_____

What is sub-vocalization, and why was it identified as an obstacle in speed reading?

_____

_____

_____

_____

_____

## Goals

What are the tools you need to use to improve your reading speed?

_____

_____

_____

_____

_____

Why is practice important in almost anything?

_____

_____

_____

_____

_____

What have you learned in this chapter that you could apply in your daily activities?

_____

_____

_____

_____

_____

1.  If you want to learn something fast and really improve, always take time to **practice**. Allot a time every day to improve a certain skill.

# Chapter 15: Thinking

Jim quotes Albert Einstein: *"We can't solve problems by using the same kind of thinking we used when we created them."* You cannot use the outdated ways of learning anymore because the accessibility of information has also changed. What you need is to be mindful of how you are going to absorb information and retain it based on different new ways. Jim says that we should think exponentially and not typically. He says that we should not think outside the box, we should think in another box altogether. This improves efficiency by around 100%.

The first technique is to think with a positive approach; allow yourself to feel it. Don't let your thinking be limited. Then, try to solve the problem by approaching it in a new way. Let your imagination run wild. According to Jim, there are different ways to measure smartness. There are musical, bodily-kinesthetic, linguistic, and many other forms of smartness. Some people are a combination of two, while some possess average qualities of all of them.

Jim also presents different mental models, which are the shortcut to decoding the world around us and make sense of everything. Mental models train your mind to think. His favorite models include the 40/70 rule that he applies for rulemaking. Another model that he likes for increasing productivity is making a not-to-do list. People make a to-do list, but Jim says that both are important. You know what you have to do and what you don't have to do. That'll keep you on track and keep the important things prioritized. For problem solving, he says that his favorite model is studying his errors. Whenever a problem occurs, be clear about what took place and what did not, then magnify and see what caused the problem, then look into its layers and spot the hidden culprit too, then learn from this incident and make sure that this problem doesn't occur again in your life. A wise man never gets bitten by a snake twice. For strategy, he says that he prefers second-order thinking. Slowly and steadily move towards your goals while executing a series of plans, and you'll eventually reach your goal.

Jim finishes the chapter by telling readers how much greatness they contain within. He says, "Love yourself, trust yourself, know yourself, be yourself." Have no ends, no endings, and no finishes, be limitless.

## *The Takeaway*

In the end, our power is defined by how much we are willing to commit to becoming limitless. There are different tools that have been presented in this book that would improve our problem-solving abilities.

*Points for Reflection*

Among the types of intelligence that Jim presented, which do you feel you could relate to?

_____

_____

_____

_____

_____

*Goals*

How do you feel about the tools you have used?

_____

_____

_____

_____

_____

When applying the De Bono Approach, what have you observed about your own problem-solving skills?

_____

_____

_____

_____

_____

What have you learned in this chapter that you could apply to your daily activities?

_____

_____

_____

_____

_____

1.  Apply the **Six Thinking Hat Approach** when trying to solve a problem and evaluate how it has contributed to your problem-solving. Write down its impact.

# Conclusion

This book has told us that there are many ways to become limitless. However, it's always up to us how we respond to the challenge. Will you continue to be limited, or are you the person who has decided to become limitless? Do you want to experience your highest potential by simply applying Jim Kwik's framework to your daily activities?

In the end, the book can only guide you and provide you with the necessary tools that you can use as you move forward with your life. These tools, although valuable, can become useless and meaningless if they are not applied. You are your own superhero with your own superpower. USE IT.

# About *Limitless: Upgrade Your Brain, Learn Anything Faster, and Unlock Your Exceptional Life*

The book, *Limitless: Upgrade Your Brain, Learn Anything Faster, And Unlock Your Exceptional Life* authored by Jim Kwik in 2020, came about as part of Jim's advocacy in mental health and global education. The book has four parts and is strategically divided based on themes. In the first part of the book, Jim gives us a baseline of the wonderful possibilities of becoming limitless. "Free your Mind" focuses on conditioning your mind to be open to the new possibilities presented in the book and how one can unleash his or her exceptional life. "The Limitless Mind (What)," "Motivation (Why)," and the "Limitless Methods (How)" make up the rest of the text. The book is packed with different insights and backed by scientific studies from other experts that Jim has worked or engaged with. The book shares a lot of promising and interesting exercises with the intention of growth and change. Not just informative but also interactive, the book can be used as a tool for learning; a skill can only be mastered with constant practice.

# Awards and Accolades

- An instant hit on the New York Times.
- Bestselling book On Wall Street Journal.
- Received acknowledgments from notable people like Will Smith.
- Appeared in news medium such as Forbes.
- Named as the 'Brain's user manual.'
- A place among the world's top brain trainers.

# About Jim Kwik

Jim Kwik has become a recognized personality in our world because of his expertise in optimizing an individual's brainpower. His story of turning his life around after suffering the impact of an accident in his childhood became one of Jim's advantages in landing himself opportunities to work with business magnates, Hollywood celebrities, political leaders, and corporate clients. His clients include Nike, SpaceX, Virgin, Google, and GE, among others.

What makes Jim stand out is being living proof that we have the power to heal ourselves and can dramatically enhance our mental performance. After deciding to change his life and win over a limited perceived notion of himself, Jim became an advocate for raising awareness in brain health and educating people about how to maximize their brain potential. He started helping individuals through brain coaching, helping one person at a time to accelerate one's brainpower.

His advocacy led him to be invited to various events to be a keynote speaker, and he was able to share his story with 200,000-person audiences annually. Apart from that, he has also produced online videos about brain health and accelerating our brain capacity as his way of reaching out to more individuals. He also started Kwik Brain, a podcast which is a consistent top-charting educational training show on iTunes, where he talks about brain health and the enormous potential of our brain by inviting experts and discussing the scientific proof that we have the ability to enhance our learning capacity regardless of our past experiences.

Since then, he has been featured by different media companies and has been a guest on different TV networks, including Forbes, HuffPost, and CNBC.

Jim is also a philanthropist, helping fund projects that are relevant to his advocacy for brain health and global education. He has donated to Alzheimer's research, having a personal connection to the disease because of his grandmother. He has also helped build schools in varying counties, providing health care, clean water, and learning for children in need. Wanting to maximize every opportunity to promote brain health and global education, Jim is also the author of *Limitless: Core Techniques to Improve Performance, Productivity, and Focus*.

# Trivia Questions

1. What did the maker of IQ tests think of his creation?
2. How can you summarize the wisdom offered in this book?
3. Has the book contributed to improving your memory?
4. Has this book inspired you to shoot for the stars? Why or why not?
5. How can a person become *Limitless*?

# Congratulations

# on finishing this workbook!

We hope that you have found this summary **valuable** and had an **enjoyable experience**.

We always **strive to improve** ourselves to **deliver the highest quality of work** to you.

But **we cannot improve without you**. If you like our efforts, **please support us** by giving us a quick review of the summary in our Amazon page by visiting the link or by scanning the QR code below. Your support will allow us to produce products of even **better quality** in the future.

https://link.intensivelife.com/LimitlessWorkbook

**Thank you!**

*The Intensive Life Publishing Team*

# About Intensive Life Publishing

We live in a fast-paced world; everyone is always doing something. We started *Intensive Life Publishing* so that we can help people ***get key ideas fast***. Our mission is to provide you with **accurate, well-written summaries** of some of the world's best-selling books so that you, as our reader, can **get the valuable information that you need**. This also, in turn, promotes those fantastic, best-selling books and their respective authors.

To know more about Intensive Life Publishing, you can visit **intensivelife.com** and **follow us** on social media:

 @intensivelifepublishing

@intensive_life

Manufactured by Amazon.ca
Bolton, ON